Grandma, is this Real Life?

Grandma,
is
this
Real
Life?

A true story of a woman
who exemplifies incredible
faith, and unconditional
love and forgiveness.

Arlane Hart

Pleasant Word

Packaged by Pleasant Word, PO Box 428, Enumclaw, WA 98022. The views expressed or implied in this work do not necessarily reflect those of Pleasant Word. The author(s) is ultimately responsible for the design, content and editorial accuracy of this work.

ISBN 1-4141-0054-X
Library of Congress Catalog Card Number: 2003113363

DEDICATED
to
My husband,
Chuck,
My children, Debbie
and Richard,
their spouses,
All my grandchildren
and
great grandchildren

In memory of my daughter Cindi
and my husband Wayne

Contents

Acknowledgements

I want to thank my wonderful husband, Chuck, for his love and support as he read the manuscript and offered valuable suggestions. To Linda Crites, for typing my handwritten notes; to Helen Pierce, for the many hours we spent together laughing and crying as she retyped and edited the manuscript; and to Judy Griffin, for her editorial touches—thank you! I couldn't have written this book without the help of these dear friends. Above all, I thank God for His faithfulness to me throughout the writing of this book and throughout my life! To God be the glory!

Foreword

Grandma, Is This Real Life? is one of the most compelling true stories you will ever read. It is a tragedy in so many ways—the murder of a woman by her husband, the loss of a child by death, two young children left to cope, a son-in-law in prison, grandparents picking up the pieces and learning to parent all over again—all entwined in one horrible incident of life. It was a testing for everyone who remained standing after the murder, but this tragedy turned into a most wonderful testimony of God's "amazing grace" in action!

In over 30 years of ministry I have never witnessed anything like it! I have been around suicides, murders by the mob, the ravages of all sorts of diseases, car wrecks, maimings, beatings and abuses, but this story tops them all! Every time I tell it, people are gripped by it. It's not so much the pain, stress and anguish that are remembered. Many people have suffered similarly. The grabber is the response to this horrendous family crisis. It will blow your mind! This is a perfect illustration of, "It's not what happens to you, but how you handle it that matters." However, in this story you will find a classic WWJD? response that will shock you, thrill you and challenge you to the core. You will not easily recover from what you are about to read.

For making a difference,
Tim Timmons
www.timtimmons.com

Introduction

*G*randma, is this *real life*? Shane whispered as our car slowly passed through the guarded gates of the prison. We had been visiting Shane's father, our son-in-law, who had killed our daughter Cindi.

His question hit me like a *bolt of lightning*! "Yes, Shane, this *is* real life, but God helps us everyday, doesn't He?

"Do you remember watching your grandpa run the hurdles in the Masters Track Meets and watching your brother, Shad, play football? Well, life is kind of like that."

Shane looked at me with puzzled eyes. "What do you mean, Grandma?"

My mind was racing. How could I explain life with all its complexities to a five-year-old boy?

"Shane, in track you run, don't you?"

"Yes, Grandma," Shane replied.

"Grandpa runs the hurdles in the track meets, remember? And every few feet he has to jump over them, right? They are high, and he has to really work hard to make it over them. It's *not* easy. Sometimes life has hurdles, too. Sometimes the hurdles—the problems—are hard to face and get through.

"Think again about your brother, Shad, who plays football. Have you ever seen him run down the field to make a touchdown with *no* opposition, Shane?"

"No, Grandma."

Well, there will be hurdles and opposition in life also. God wants to help us along life's journey. We all face troubles, but we can ask God to help us everyday, and He does! Do you understand?"

"Yes, Grandma, I kinda do."

Shane yawned and curled up beside me. He laid his head on my lap and quickly dozed off to dreamland.

CHAPTER 1

Real Life Begins

Born in my grandparents' home to Arland W. Palmer and Ruth Alva McIntosh Palmer, my "real life" began in Kansas City, Missouri, at 2458 Indiana Avenue. I was their first child, but I did have a half-brother, Perry Alva, from my mother's previous marriage.

April 10, 1930, was the momentous day. What happened between my birth and third year I haven't the slightest notion, but I vividly remember our move to California when I was about three years old. Our very old car frequently broke down along the highway.

Perry stayed in Missouri with our grandparents, Perry Alva and Ruth Ann McIntosh. I even forgot that I had a brother!

Both of my parents worked at menial jobs, mostly as market attendants. I recall staying in our small apartment in Santa Ana for hours alone entertaining myself with toys and playing house with my dolls. Grandma—

I called her Nanny—sent me clothes for my dolls. I would wash the clothes daily, hang them on the porch to dry, and play with other toys while my parents worked.

Many times Mama would leave lunch for me and then go back to work. I could never swallow the meat that she fried, so I would chew and chew and then spit it behind the table on the floor. She would come home about 4:00 p.m. and see all the tiny pieces of dried meat. She thought they were rat droppings. I never told her my secret.

I knew that my parents loved me very much. I was a happy child and took each day as it came. Arda and Fricka were my make-believe friends. I talked to them constantly and was very content playing all day with my invisible friends. They were the only friends that I had during this stage of my life!

At this time our country was deep in the throes of the depression. We moved in with friends of my parents in Santa Ana, California, to help share expenses. I loved it because the friends had a daughter my age, and I now had a *real* friend.

I thought this family was very rich because every morning the milkman left milk and eggs at their back door. Once in a while we would even get *chocolate* milk! What a treat! We would follow the milk truck and pick up the ice on the street—dirt and all!

CHAPTER 2

Early Years

My grandfather, Perry Alva McIntosh, a stockbroker, committed suicide in 1936 after losing his entire estate. My grandmother, Ruth, was left penniless. Grandfather did own three homes, however, two of which were in California. So my father, mother and I moved into a small one-bedroom home at 1622 West 2nd Street in Santa Ana, California. Within the year my grandmother and Perry, my brother who was now ten years old, joined us in this small home.

Having a brother was very new to me. My father was not kind to him, and it was evident that neither Perry nor my grandmother was welcome. My father, out of necessity, built two small bedrooms onto the back of the house to accommodate our larger family.

NELLIE

When I was seven years old, Nellie Lou, my sister, was born. Mama was extremely upset when she discovered she was pregnant. My mother and father were very unhappy together. Mama even tried to abort Nellie by taking pills and falling downstairs, but Nellie—blonde, blue-eyed, beautiful—was born on March 1, 1937. Nellie had a heart murmur and glandular problems. My parents talked about her as if she would not live very long. I worried about this much of the time.

Mama seldom attended any of my functions at school because she was afraid to leave Nellie with anyone. Babysitters were unheard of in those days, so my father almost always attended my school activities alone. Later, he was the one who took me to church regularly.

Our family never went on a vacation, never went out to eat, and almost never went anywhere together.

The house did not seem crowded to me, but I'm sure it must have been. The property fronted on 2nd street and reached through to 1st street, which was a main thoroughfare in the early 1930s and is still quite busy.

Daddy built a small shed and started a fruit and vegetable stand business on 1st Street. He and Perry worked at least eight hours a day, seven days a week. Mama shelled walnuts and raised chickens to sell to neighbors and teachers. Her hands were stained black from the walnut hulls.

Daddy was on W.P.A. (Works Progress Administration), a government program to help the poorer people. I wore allotment dresses. My mother would remake them to fit, and she would put new buttons on them so they barely resembled the ones my girlfriends were wearing.

I was unaware of the struggle my parents were facing during this time of my life. A loaf of bread was 10 cents. I remember Mama begging Daddy for a dime!

KINDERGARTEN

My first day of kindergarten was so exciting! My teacher sat at a big brown box with white and black things coming out the front. All she did was wriggle her fingers over these and out came beautiful music! I wanted to dance, but she would say, "Arlane, please go lie down on your mat." I didn't want to, but of course I did.

After school I ran home excitedly. "Mama, the teacher has this wonderful big brown box that makes music."

My mother quickly realized what I was talking about and told me it was a PIANO and laughed.

"Will I ever be able to play the piano?"

"I'm sorry, Arlane. You see, pianos are expensive. We will never be able to buy you a piano. Besides, you would have to take lessons. They are expensive, too. No, you will never have a piano! Please don't mention it again!"

Well, that didn't keep me from wishing. I loved school and could hardly wait to hear the piano. Every day at home, I would pretend I was playing the piano on our dining table. My parents would scold me for ignoring my meals to play my pretend piano.

I also loved to sing. One of my favorite things to do was to sit with my father, while he attended the fruit stand, and sing familiar songs. Christmas songs were my favorite, and we sang these all year around. Even in the second grade, I could harmonize with my father.

FOURTH OF JULY

One Fourth of July someone gave our family tickets to attend the celebration at the Santa Ana Bowl. We were all tremendously excited! This was the only event we had ever planned to attend together. My brother, Perry, who was about 12 at the time, was working in the fruit stand and had to run to the house for change. He hurried around the corner of the garage and ran into little Nellie, who was about 1°, knocking her into the air. I saw her land on her head. My parents were certain she had suffered a concussion and rushed her to the hospital, leaving me behind crying my eyes out! We were so relieved when the doctors told us she was not seriously injured, but we didn't attend the Fourth of July celebration that evening.

CHRISTMAS

Christmas was always interesting at our house. Mama tied branches of fir trees together and somehow created a Christmas tree. We always thought it was beautiful. Sometimes we wouldn't see the tree until Christmas morning.

One Christmas, Mama earned about $20 selling walnuts and chickens from our backyard. We were all so happy. Santa brought me a beautiful doll that year.

I can never remember receiving more than one or two gifts at Christmas time. I loved Christmas, however, because we always had a big Christmas dinner. We had fried chicken from our backyard and olives and sometimes soup. Mama baked bread, and the W.P.A. furnished the butter!

GLIMPSES OF CHILDHOOD

Sometimes my father would take *only me* to the malt shop downtown and buy me a malt. They were so delicious, and they were only 10 cents each. We would sit and talk. He would tell me not to tell Perry—he *never* took Perry. Those were special times for me, but I felt so sorry for my brother. Perry would smell my breath and go off and cry.

School was fun for me. The subjects seemed to be easy, and I was almost always the teacher's pet. I played violin duets with the principal and was the emcee for plays and special programs in the auditorium. I made good grades and enjoyed doing extra work for better grades.

In the sixth grade I was able to buy a used bicycle for $10. I had saved five cents a week since kindergarten, and I could finally pay for it. Mama painted it blue and white. I rode my bike to Willard Junior High School daily, about five miles each way.

I was shy in junior high. The school was so big, and there were hundreds of kids. I felt inferior but still worked hard.

When I was 13, we moved to 727 South Birch Street in Santa Ana. This was a much better neighborhood, and we were closer to Lathrop Junior High and Santa Ana High School.

My brother went into the service when he was 17, and then to college at San Jose State. He later married Shirley and moved to Northern California. They had two children,

Sheryl and Mark. We rarely saw each other until we were adults with families of our own. We now see him once or twice a year. He is married to his second wife, Margaret, who has three daughters. They are very happy.

My mother was extremely talented musically. As a young woman she was a concert violinist. She played several different instruments and was even an orchestra leader. She learned to play the piano without any lessons. I thought she was a genius. She epitomized the term "flapper" and won numerous dance contests during her youth.

CHAPTER 3

A Life-Changing Week

When Nanny, my grandmother, moved in with us, she saw me enthusiastically playing the table and asked my mother what I was doing. Mama told her I thought I was playing a *piano*. She came over, sat down beside me, and asked, "Do you really like the piano, Arlane?" Of course I responded with a hearty, "YES!" She immediately told me she would like to buy a piano for me. WHAT A THRILL!

Early the next Saturday morning Nanny, Mama and I walked to town. The only music company in town was the "Blue Note Music Co." on 4th Street. The salesman led us to the backroom and pointed to a very large brown piano. Some of the ivory tops of the keys were missing, and the material behind the carving was all punched in. It looked very old, but it was beautiful to me. My heart was pounding hard. Was this piano going to be mine?

Within a few moments my grandmother gave the man $25. He lifted me onto the round piano stool and announced that the piano was mine. I couldn't believe it. My dream had come true. I had a *piano*!

In a few days the large piano was delivered to our home. Out went the davenport, and in came my piano!

Mama sat right down and played "Happy Birthday." How, I do not know! She later picked up many pieces of sheet music at Goodwill for five cents each. As a family we would stand around the piano and sing such songs as "Long, Long Trail," "Laugh, Clown, Laugh" and "Five Foot Two."

My grandmother, who once taught piano and was an excellent pianist herself, told me she would teach me how to play the piano. She brought out a book called *Teaching Little Fingers to Play*. She sat with me daily as I progressed through the book. I loved every minute of it. Nanny would reward me with a dime for having a good lesson!

I began to improve daily. All of my spare waking hours were spent at the piano, playing out of books and composing my own little pieces. I remember listening to the radio and trying to copy the songs I heard. "Major Bowes Original Amateur Hour" was my favorite radio program.

My parents were both wonderful encouragers. They would stand in the doorway and clap when I finished a piece. Daddy was my greatest critic. Even though he had never studied music, he had a great ear and would tell me when a note was wrong or the timing was off. He had a very good singing voice, too. Whenever friends or company would come to our house, I always had to play the piano for them. Mama would say many times, "Either help me with the dishes or practice the piano." Guess what I did!

One day, Nanny announced that she was moving away. I was grief-stricken! She was getting married. Well the piano lessons left, too. I struggled to teach myself, but it didn't work very well. A little girlfriend helped me a bit, but I struggled with learning and progressing the way I wanted to. I played a few songs by listening to the radio and trying to copy them, but my piano playing basically came to a standstill with no one to teach me.

CHAPTER 4

Vacation Bible School

I was about ten years old, still desiring to play the piano better, trying to teach myself, when I happened to be walking home from the school grounds of Franklin Elementary in Santa Ana. I had been occupying my long summer hours by doing tricks on the hand bars, jumping rope with friends, playing jacks—the usual things a child does on a hot summer day—when I decided to walk home alone.

As I left the playground I heard the sounds of a piano! The music was coming from a small church on the corner which I had never noticed before. I attended church very little at that time of my life, just a few weddings and funerals. Once in a while I went to Sunday School at the United Methodist Church, but I never really understood why churches existed.

I walked slowly toward the building and up the steps. The doors were open. There was a big sign on the front that said, "VACATION BIBLE SCHOOL." I went in and sat down on a seat in the back. Up in the front near the pulpit, a blonde teenaged girl was seated at a piano. I had never heard such beautiful music. Even my kindergarten teacher didn't play that well!

I sat there mesmerized for at least an hour. Finally she stood up and spoke to me. "Hi. Do you like the piano?"

I answered very shyly, "I love the piano."

She invited me to come on down, and I jumped at the chance. We became acquainted. Her name was Murella Schliebe, and could she play the piano! Murella told me that she was practicing for Vacation Bible School.

"What's that?" I questioned.

She explained that during the summer the church had a week's program for boys and girls like me. They sang, played games, listened to Bible stories, and just had fun!

"Wow. Could I come?" I really wanted to since *she* was going to be playing the piano every day that week.

Before we parted, she also explained to me that she was starting to teach piano, and she would love to have me as her very first student. She would charge me 50 cents for all afternoon, every Sunday!

I was overjoyed at this news and could hardly wait to tell my daddy. I ran home so fast to tell him the good news. Daddy looked down at me very sadly and explained he could not afford 50 cents. I began to cry and started to walk away. He could see my disappointment. "Ask her if she'd do it for a quarter," he suggested.

I ran back to the church and asked her, and she said, "Yes!" We hugged each other and danced around the piano—laughing with joy!

I could hardly wait until Monday morning to see my new friend and hear her play the piano. I awoke very early, put on my favorite summer dress, and anxiously waited for 9:00 a.m. to arrive. The church was only two blocks from my home, and I hurried toward the building that would be instrumental in changing my life forever!

The church was bursting with kids of all ages. They were laughing, running, talking, and having so much fun. What a wonderful experience to be a part of this exciting activity!

A teacher led me into a small classroom with about 10 other children. She quietly took her place in front of the group as she asked, "Do you know that the God who created the universe loves YOU?" She looked straight at me!

I had never even thought about God, much less that He loved *me*. She continued, "Do you know that we all are born with sin in our lives?" I listened closely, wondering what sin was.

"Sin is anything that separates us from God. It can be a bad action or a bad thought." For the first time in my life, I realized I was a sinner.

"Because God loves us so much, He wants us to live with Him in heaven one day. So He sent His only Son, Jesus, into this world. He lived on this earth and then, as a young man, He was crucified on a cross and died for the sins of the world." He died for MY sins. I cried. I was so sorry for the wrong things I had done.

The teacher said that if we tell Him we are sorry and ask Him to forgive us, He will!

She also explained that Jesus rose from the grave three days later and lives in heaven with God. That made me very happy. "Jesus will live in our hearts if we ask Him."

I wanted Jesus to live in my heart, so that very moment I bowed my head and said a simple prayer and invited Him into my life. The prayer went something like this, "Dear Jesus, I'm sorry for all the wrong things I've done. Please forgive me. Right now I open my heart's door and invite You to come into my heart. Thank you for giving me eternal life. Please make me the kind of person you want me to be. Amen." My walk with Him began that moment.

Vacation Bible School was even better than I expected. I learned so many songs that week: "Oh, How I Love Jesus," "The B-I-B-L-E," "I Have the Joy, Joy, Joy, Joy, Down in My Heart," and, of course, "Jesus Loves Me." The Bible stories were great! I remember receiving a prize for memorizing the most Bible verses that week.

"Jesus is the same, yesterday, today and forever" (Hebrews 13:8).

"God is Love" (1 John 4:8).

"For God so loved the world that He gave his only begotten Son, that whosoever believes in Him should not perish but have everlasting life" (John 3:16).

"Trust in the LORD with all your heart, and lean not on your own understanding; in all your ways acknowledge Him, and He shall direct your paths" (Proverbs 3:5–6).

Truly, He has directed my path.

Sunday, just like Murella promised, she arrived at my home about 1:00 p.m. and stayed until 5:00 p.m. She brought the church hymnal instead of a "boring" methods book and taught me right out of the hymnal. We had so much fun. She taught me most of the chords that summer. Each week I progressed. We played, sang, and became friends—real friends.

By the time I was 11 or 12 years old, I was playing the piano for children's groups at church. I had wonderful friends in this church. My parents and sister, Nellie, all began to attend that little First Assembly of God Church on 3rd Street in Santa Ana.

CHAPTER 5

A Lesson Well Learned

$\mathcal{E}$llen McAfee was one of my very best friends. When I was about 11, she was 13. She was much wiser than I in many ways, and I idolized her. When she said sit, I sat. When she had an idea, I followed her leading. She was an only child, and we attended the same little church where I met Jesus. We were inseparable to say the least!

One summer day we, or should I say she, decided we should walk to town and go shopping. How fun that would be! So I approached my father. He was not too thrilled with the idea but reluctantly gave his approval since Ellen seemed to be quite mature in every way. He felt she would watch over me.

Daddy gave me $3 to buy a purse I had wanted for a long time, and off we went. Santa Ana had a very nice store called Rankins. Ellen wanted to shop there first, and so we did.

While we were in Rankins, we decided to use the restroom. It was empty except for two large packages under the sink. We both were curious and proceeded to unwrap the packages. I felt guilty but decided if Ellen thought it was okay, it must be okay!

Inside the wrappings were men's overalls. The large package had a price tag of $15, and the smaller one a price tag of $11. Ellen was excited. I questioned her, thinking we would just turn them in to the lost-and-found department, but Ellen had something else in mind. She suggested we go to Penney's to return the overalls saying they did not fit our fathers. Penney's would then give us the money for them.

I felt terrible. I knew this was totally wrong, but I did it. She went first and came running out of the store all smiles saying, "Arlane, it is so easy! Just tell them what I told you to say, and in a few minutes you will have $11 in your hands!"

It was the hardest thing I had ever done. The clerk looked at me very curiously and said, "Goodness, you are the second one today who is returning overalls! This is very strange. But, okay, I will give you the $11."

With the money in my hands I returned to Ellen and tried to act happy, but I was really miserable. We went straight back to Rankins, where she bought a black negligee. She said she had always dreamed of having one. I thought it looked silly.

Our next stop was the shoe store to buy the purse I wanted. To my disappointment, the purse wasn't there, but there was another one almost like the one that I wanted. It was $4 instead of $3. I bought it and hid the rest of the money in my socks.

At the dinner table that evening my father asked to see the purse that I had bought. I ran to my bedroom to get it. I was very nervous for fear he would start asking questions, and he did. When he examined the purse, the price tag was still on it. The $4 was big and clear.

"Arlane, I thought that you said that this purse was $3. Where did you get the extra dollar?" I lied and probably turned very red. "It was on sale, Daddy."

Then I began to cry and told him everything that had happened that day.

"Arlane, you know what you have to do, don't you?"

"What, Daddy?" I sobbed.

"You have to take the purse back tomorrow and return all of the money that you stole from Penney's."

I couldn't sleep that night. The next day my father and I walked to town. We tried to take Ellen with us, but her folks felt she did not need to go.

We returned the purse and made our way to Penney's. Daddy asked to speak to the manager of the store before I was brought to his office upstairs.

I gave him the money as I told him the story, crying all the time. He gave me a lecture that I will never forget and said goodbye to me. I was so glad to go home without the purse or money.

The day I turned 16 years old my father awakened me with, "Today, I want you to put on your best dress and shoes, comb your hair neatly, scrub your face and come with me." We walked downtown once again to JC Penney's. We stood out in front and he said, "Now go inside and ask for the manager, you know, the one you had to face when you were

11 years old. He will not recognize you, but I want you to tell him who you are and remind him of the incident five years ago. Tell him that you need a job and ask him if there are any openings in the store."

"Oh, Daddy, I can't do that. I am still so ashamed, I can't. Please don't make me do that." But I did.

The manager was very nice and did remember the "overall incident." His first question was, "Are you good at math?"

"Yes, I am," I shyly replied.

He gave me a test and arose from his chair. "Come with me, Arlane. We need a cashier for the entire store, and I believe you can fill that job!"

I was overwhelmed. "How do I do that?"

He explained, "All of the money downstairs on the selling floor comes to the second floor by way of little cups that are clipped onto electric cords. You will receive those cups with the money on the second floor, make the change and send them back to the clerks. We will train you for this job. How does that sound?"

I reported for work the next day and held that job all summer and on Saturdays during the school year.

I learned a very important lesson, thanks to my father!

CHAPTER 6

Family Vacations

During my childhood we never went on vacation. My parents could barely buy food and clothing! I'm sure that many families were that way in the 1930s. Just surviving was the "way of life" then. Life was hard!

The 1940s were a bit better. We were still never able to leave the house to relax, but we did acquire a refrigerator and a telephone during this time!

My first vacation was with Wayne the first summer we were married. Wayne was a very adventurous young man, and we decided to go to Sequoia National Park for a few days. We brought a small tent and ate canned food. Our drive home ended with a head-on collision. The car was totaled, and I was hospitalized. My nose was broken, my teeth were all dislodged, and my upper lip was badly cut. The scar still reminds me of our first vacation. Needless to say, I wasn't too anxious to travel by car for the next few years.

Two years after we were married, Cindy was born. We spent a few weeks in Santa Ana with our parents. Wayne always had a summer job in Orange County, and it was a big relief to escape from the Bakersfield heat.

Later, when we had three small children under the age of four, we would take off for Missouri the day school was out to visit Wayne's sister Viola and her family. We would stay about two weeks and then drive home. Often we brought another person back to California with us. We did this yearly until the children started to complain about the long trips in the small backseat of our car.

Some of our vacations were then spent with other families. The Jay Reed family and the Ed Murphy family joined us many times to vacation in the mountains or national parks. We brought tents and camping supplies and cooked our food on an open fire or stayed in friends' cabins in the mountains. The Finns, Burtons, and Stifflers also joined us many times.

As the children grew older they suggested renting a beach house at Newport for a week in the summer. We did this for about five years. We had to save all year for this exciting week. Our family enjoyed this very much, and we kept this tradition until the children left the nest.

CHAPTER 7

Junior High, High School And College

JUNIOR HIGH AND HIGH SCHOOL

When I was about 13 years old and very bashful, my mom, dad, sister and I were all seated in church when the song leader stood and asked, "Can anyone in the audience play the piano?" My mother, who was not bashful, put her hand to my back and nearly pushed me out of the seat, "Get up there and play the piano, Arlane. We've spent at least four dollars on your lessons." Well, I obeyed Mama, sat on that piano bench, and have never gotten off!

Thirteen was a wonderful year. The piano played a big part of my life. The kids enjoyed my playing, I enjoyed it, and my mom and dad loved to hear me play. In fact, one day during summer vacation, Daddy suggested I start teaching piano to young children to earn some money for my clothes and other expenses. I balked at first but started thinking about it and decided to try it. So, riding my $10 bike, I went out to find a few students. I did find some children in my neighborhood who had pianos and started my career. I charged 50 cents for all afternoon, and some children actually learned to play! I have continued teaching until this present day with much success.

TEENAGE YEARS

After moving across town to South Birch Street, my father and I began to attend a small neighborhood church called the Gospel Center. There were only five young people in this church. One of the boys was Dean Lovass. I later became engaged to Dean during my freshman year at Santa Ana College. I played the piano for some of the services at the church and sang solos occasionally. I was a friend of everyone in the church, especially the young couples. They all had quite an influence on me as to the choice of a lifetime mate. What great examples they were.

At the age of 16, I was allowed to date but was afraid. I did not want to go out, but one young man persisted and I did go to a movie with him. We walked, of course. I had to be home by 10:00 p.m. Those were very happy days.

I forgot to mention that in our home we never turned lights on unless it was an emergency. I could keep a light on over the piano in the evening if I practiced. Once I quit practicing, however, the light went out and I was off to bed. So I practiced every evening—late!

We also never made long-distance phone calls. One day I phoned my girlfriend Shirley in Orange but did not know it was long distance. The phone bill, of course, showed five cents more the following month. My father flew into a rage and said, "DON'T YOU EVER MAKE A LONG DISTANCE CALL ON MY PHONE AGAIN!" I never did, and I'm extremely cautious to this day about the phone bill.

I began working in different stores in downtown Santa Ana, taking the bus to work. I was a cashier at Penney's, a sales clerk at various stores, and a credit application clerk at Sears. I saved enough money to go away to college. Daddy told me over and over again he could not afford to pay for my college education but if I really wanted to go, I would find a way. During this time I paid room and board to him and saved like crazy because I really wanted to go to college.

High school was exciting. There were football games, choir concerts, Mary's Malt Shop and the "Happy Days" gang, but my studies came first. I made the Honor Roll almost every semester. The piano was especially fun because I was allowed to play all the popular songs. Kids loved to stand behind me at the piano and sing. I was the regular pianist at the Gospel Center church in Santa Ana. I enjoyed working part-time in some of the department stores in downtown Santa Ana.

I graduated from Santa Ana High School in June 1948. I spent most of my free time at Newport and Balboa beaches. We all had beautiful tans and didn't worry about skin cancer in those days.

COLLEGE

Santa Ana College was my next educational step. I took the usual courses every freshman takes, and I was the accompanist for the voice class. A young man by the name of Wayne Ambrose was a student in that class. We became acquainted. By the time I had finished the year at Santa Ana College, I had saved enough money to go away to college. I had accomplished this by working afternoons and Saturdays at Sears and by eating peanut butter sandwiches on the bus on the way to work.

My favorite subjects were the music courses, naturally!

FIRST DATE

One morning after Voice 1-A class, Wayne and I were walking towards the Student Center. Wayne jokingly approached me with, "Do you go to shows?" Immediately I remembered my childhood church. The people there were strongly against movies. Anything to do with Hollywood was wrong. Could he be one of those? I was curious but quickly replied, "Sure." I surprised myself.

"Maybe we could go sometime," he suggested.

"Okay," I answered.

We climbed the steps to the student center and greeted other friends. He sat down beside me.

"How about going with me to a beach party Saturday night?"

"What happened to the movie?" I asked.

He laughed. He always laughed. We set a time for the beach party, and we parted.

Saturday night came. He didn't show up at the time he said, and I felt he had "stood me up." I'd never had that happen before. My mother was furious. She felt I should never see this young man again.

I had changed into my bedclothes when around 9:00 p.m. there was a heavy jolt on our front porch that rocked the house and a loud ring of the doorbell.

He laughed as he explained his tardiness. I changed back into my beach attire, said goodbye to Mom, and left with Wayne. We laughed our way to the car. There were two other couples already in the car, neither of whom I knew. The boys were casual friends of Wayne's from the track team. The car was very old. Both headlights were out. I had to sit on a pile of firewood in the back seat and banged my head on the roof of the car. Everyone, including Wayne, was very loud. I wanted to go home. I was absolutely miserable.

We drove about five miles on dark side streets, hoping a cop wouldn't catch us, when all of a sudden there was a terrible jolt and the car came to a screeching halt. We were all tossed about in the car. The girls screamed, the boys yelled.

We piled out to investigate. To our surprise, we were in a bean field. The front tires were both blown out. We had hit a barricade. Well, that was the beginning and end of our beach party. The other two couples left to seek help, and Wayne and I stayed by the car. All we could do was talk.

"Where are you going to college next year?" he inquired.

"I've been accepted at Redlands," I replied.

"Why Redlands?"

'Well, it's small, close to home but not too close, and I think it's a Christian college. I *really* want to attend a Christian college."

He picked up on that fast. "A church college, huh?" Have you ever heard of Pasadena College?" he asked.

"No," I answered.

Well, for the next hour I heard all about Pasadena College. It sounded wonderful. It was exactly what I was looking for.

Wayne explained he was a junior and was just picking up some lower division units this semester. I was impressed. His desire was to be a high school coach and teacher, and he would be returning to Pasadena College in September.

I found out that Wayne was a born-again Christian and an outstanding athlete with a goal in life. Besides that he had an outgoing, fun-loving personality. All of my friends liked him.

COLLEGE AND WAYNE

That evening was a turning point in my life. I felt God's plan was being unveiled. I felt good about our relationship. In a few weeks I withdrew my transcripts from Redlands and sent them to Pasadena!

My junior year of college was in Pasadena. I had saved enough money from different jobs to completely pay for the next year. It was a wonderful year, and I met lifetime friends. It was at Pasadena College where I totally surrendered my life to Christ and established a real goal about my music also. I knew then that I wanted to teach, perform, and be used in any way God wanted to use me. I felt His hand totally upon me.

I played the piano for a small radio program in Orange, California, at that time. The director was my first piano teacher, Murella Schliebe. I thoroughly enjoyed it and earned a small salary during those days at Pasadena College.

Wayne was the only child in his family at that time who had graduated from high school, much less college. He was born in Arkansas into a large family of 11 children. He was right in the middle. He claims that he was always referred to as "Hey, you!" He told many humorous stories of his childhood. He could entertain his friends for hours with his funny childhood experiences and corny jokes.

Because his family was so poor, he was placed in the foster home of a Free Methodist pastor. To earn his keep, he was the church janitor and groundskeeper. He was required to listen to classical music for an hour each day. He attended a Christian high school, spent two years in the Naval Air Corps, and then went on to Pasadena College where he graduated in 1950.

The first time Wayne heard that God loved him was from a truck driver who picked him up while he was hitchhiking and told him about Jesus. He turned his life over to Jesus that day.

I loved his family right from the start. They were all friendly, outgoing and fun. Never had I been around such a large group of family members. They had wonderful Sunday dinners and picnics. Their family was totally opposite from my family. We never had anyone over for dinner. My folks had very few friends and never seemed to have very much to eat.

It was during this time I decided that I wanted to raise my future children in that kind of atmosphere—free, relaxed, happy, giving. My parents found it hard to accept this and thought we were crazy and irresponsible at times, but they gradually learned to accept my new way of life.

Wayne was an outstanding coach and athlete. He took a personal interest in his boys and spent numerous hours outside of school with his students. His teams nearly always won due to his excellent coaching and personal attention.

After we were married, our home was continually open to his athletes. It was not unusual to have two or three extra mouths to feed at dinnertime or even to have overnight guests. Our weekends were usually spent at the beach with boys and girls from the church and track or football teams for a wiener roast or barbeque in our backyard.

OUR WEDDING

Wayne and I were engaged in June 1950 and married on August 31 of the same year at the Church of Nazarene in Santa Ana.

Our wedding cost approximately $200, which I had saved during the summer. We borrowed $20 from Wayne's brother Olin to go on our honeymoon.

I made my wedding gown—10 yards of satin, a yard of lace, no pattern—for $10. I copied it after Elizabeth Taylor's dress that she wore in "The Father of the Bride" on the cover of *Bride Magazine*. It was a beautiful wedding, reception and all. More than 200 people attended.

Wayne and I both continued school the next year. He attended graduate school at Los Angeles State, and I picked up some units at Pasadena City College. I worked all during my college years at Sears in the credit department. Wayne also worked at various jobs.

CHAPTER 8

On To Life

Wayne's first official coaching job was in Bakersfield at a junior high school. It was while we were in Bakersfield that our two little girls were born, Cindy on November 21, 1952, and Debbie on April 19, 1955. They were such a joy, beautiful and healthy. Praise God!

Wayne became the youth director in the church. Ours was a busy household.

I learned to drive during this period of my life because of serious dental problems and frequent trips to the dentist. We only had one car.

We left Bakersfield every June to escape the heat and returned in September. We were also a bit homesick for our parents who lived in Santa Ana.

When Cindy was six months old, Murella, my childhood piano teacher, called me. "Arlane, would you like to fill in for me playing the organ during the summer on Lido Isle at Richard's Market?"

I was shocked to hear her voice and replied, "Murella, I don't even play the organ."

"Just get to one at a skating rink or funeral home. You can do it."

Well, if she thought I could, I guess I could! She had great faith in me.

So I called all the funeral homes and found one about four miles from our home which would allow me to practice. My love for the organ began. I had not learned to drive yet and we only had one car anyway, so I put Cindy in her little buggy along with her food, cloth diapers, and other supplies for the day and took off walking over the bridge into Bakersfield. The funeral director was amazed that I had come all that way with a baby. He carried the baby and buggy up a flight of stairs and ushered me into the organ chamber.

I had no idea what to do with that huge instrument, but I soon found out. The instruction books were in the bench, and I began to study and teach myself. Cindy and I would travel to town two or three days each week so I could practice on that organ.

I auditioned for the job at Richard's Market with Richard himself during Easter week and was hired. The pay was $10 an hour. I felt like a millionaire!

When we returned to Bakersfield after that first summer, the church had purchased an organ. I was appointed organist and was quite pleased with the position.

Wayne and I were both getting tired of the heat in summer and the cold in the winter (me, mostly) and we also wanted to come back to Orange County (me, mostly) where our families were, so he applied for a coaching

job in Garden Grove and was hired. We packed our belongings and moved back to Southern California with
our two darling daughters, 1° and 3 years old.

Our families were overjoyed to have us all home again,
and we purchased a small home on Mac Street in Garden
Grove with Wayne's G.I. Bill. We paid $13,000 for the
house. Rancho Alamitos High School, where Wayne was
to begin his new job, was only five blocks away.

We both became very active in the Garden Grove
Nazarene Church. He was youth director and Sunday
school teacher, and I was pianist/organist and choir director. Our son, Richard, was born during this time, on
April 5, 1957. We were delighted to have a boy.

Our lives continued to be extremely active. We moved
from the Mac Street house a few years later to a new,
lovely home on Laird Street in Santa Ana, just on the
outskirts of Garden Grove. We paid $21,000 for this
home, a huge amount of money for a teacher. I started
teaching piano lessons again to supplement our income.
We were a typical American family.

During these years, we housed about 24 young
people. Some stayed with us a few weeks, others a few
months, and others even years. These young people were
usually unhappy in their own home situation and sought
refuge in our home. All were boys except for Jane, who
came to us during her sophomore year in high school.
She was a drug pusher, and her parents were going wild
with her problem. She came in September and left the
following June. She became a believer and attended
church regularly with our family. Ultimately she returned
to her home in Costa Mesa. Her parents also came to

51

know Jesus during this time. That summer she attended a church camp, met one of the park laborers, and came home pregnant. She named her little girl Cindy. When her Cindy was about 1° years old, Jane was found dead along the side of the road near San Francisco from an overdose of drugs. We were devastated.

We have a story about each person who stayed with us. One boy, Jim Wilson, went on to Bible College and became a minister of the Gospel.

During these years my mother, Ruth Palmer, became ill with lymphoma. We were very close. She was quite a woman, and we had a wonderful relationship. I was able to lead her to the Lord on her deathbed as I held her tiny head in my arms and released her to the Lord on February 14, 1975.

God was truly my strength at this time. I felt total peace and joy. This was the first time I had experienced the loss of a close family member. God was there, and my faith was strengthened. When I am weak, He is strong!

Two years later, my father, Arland W. Palmer, passed away at the age of 79. I had the privilege of reading to him from the Bible daily and also being with him during his death. He was an encourager and a wise father. I loved him very much. He was never able to give me much materially, but he gave me things far more valuable—his time and his wisdom. He passed away in a rest home in Santa Ana from what I believe was Alzheimer's and pneumonia. He was very calm and peaceful in death.

BACK TO COLLEGE

Ten years after Wayne and I were married, I returned to college. I enrolled at Fullerton State and then attended Long Beach State the following year. I completed the coursework and was granted a provisional credential to teach in the elementary schools of Garden Grove.

I applied for substitute teaching and taught nearly every day for a year. For the next four years, I taught Release Time Education in the Orange Elementary District. That was a wonderful experience! I taught Bible to fourth and fifth graders who were released from their classes. My pay was equivalent to a regular substitute teacher, and my rewards were many. I had the opportunity to lead many children to the Lord during those four years.

CHRISTIAN WOMEN'S CLUB

Even though my life was extremely busy, I had a great desire to become involved in the Christian Women's Club. I learned of this organization through an ad in the paper and attended my first meeting in 1958. I put the children in the club's nursery and instantly became very active. The women in the Garden Grove Club became dear friends, and to this day I see several of them monthly for lunch.

Christian Women's Club is the outreach of Stonecroft Ministries. Over the years, I have invited many neighbors and acquaintances to attend the luncheons where they have accepted Christ as their personal Savior.

In 1973 I founded the Huntington Beach Club and became their first chairman, a responsibility I held for two years.

I served as an Area Representative for many years and was Chairman of the Southern California/Arizona Conference in 1983 in Los Angeles.

It has been my privilege since 1991 to be a speaker for this organization, giving my testimony all over the United States. I am so grateful and count it a real honor to be a part of this great organization.

DEBBIE

Debbie's health was not good after she contracted the German measles at the age of three. Her kidneys were damaged, and she was in the hospital many times with four or five surgeries. She kept us on our knees. We prayed for hours for her healing. She was a beautiful little girl and kept us chuckling with all of her cute sayings. Debbie accepted Jesus at a young age. She came home one Sunday from church crying hysterically. She wanted to be baptized as soon as possible, so she called our pastor and made arrangements for the following week. Debbie was very serious about her relationship with God. Debbie had and still has a very straightforward way about her. She is a very truthful person and can't handle deceitfulness in other people.

Debbie is extremely artistic and creative. Now, as an adult, she owns and operates Ambrosia Interiors, a very successful design center. Her role as a mother is demanding, but she seems to almost miraculously manage her household and her work outside the home.

RICHARD

After having two girls, our hearts' desire was to have a little boy. We anxiously awaited the birth of our third child. During my sixth month of pregnancy, I participated in a nationwide test. My doctor, Dr. Richard McDonald, assured me it was only about 80% accurate, but I went ahead with the test. My saliva would indicate whether I would have a boy or a girl. He submitted it for the experiment.

We did not have a telephone. I gave the doctor my neighbor's number so he could call me with the test results. Both Wayne and I were extremely excited anticipating the outcome of the test.

Early one morning my neighbor knocked on our door. "It's your doctor, Arlane. He wants to talk to you."

I know that I was shaking when I put the receiver to my ear. He explained that the test results were in and he was about to give me the long-awaited news.

"What do you have now, Arlane?" he questioned.

"I have two darling little girls," I answered.

"Well, Arlane, it looks like you are going to have a BOY this time, but don't be too excited as you know it is not 100% accurate.

I shouted and cried with joy, "A BOY, a BOY, how wonderful!"

The next three months were the longest three months of my entire life. Finally the day came.

On April 5, 1957, Richard Bryce Ambrose was born. He weighed 7 pounds, 14 ounces and was 19 inches long. We praised God for this gift of love.

We nicknamed him Dickie. He was our bundle of joy. Dickie was mild-tempered, cute as they come, and gave our family much pleasure. As he grew he warmed our hearts with his loving manner and sweet spirit. He never complained about anything. Once when he was riding his bicycle, the paper boy ran into him and knocked him down. He remarked that his arm hurt a little. Two weeks went by and he again reminded me that his arm still hurt. I took him finally to the doctor and found out he had broken his arm. I felt terrible!

Another time when he was about 9 years old, he said he felt very tired. I remarked it was summer and all of us felt a little tired because of the heat. Again we visited the doctor and discovered he had double pneumonia! I wanted to crawl under the table. I felt like a terrible mother.

Dickie took trumpet lessons and was very good. When he entered junior high school, he was first trumpeter in the school orchestra. He continued to play until his sisters made so much fun of him that he quit. Poor Dickie, he had to put up with a lot from his sisters.

Dickie was introduced to Donna Franks by his sisters one day. They became sweethearts and, to our surprise, they eloped! Donna had a two-year-old boy, Curtis. Richard later adopted him, and in a few years they had a little girl named Heather.

Richard has been steadily employed first by Smart & Final and later as a car salesman with the Chrysler Corporation.

He is no longer the quiet little boy I once knew. Donna says he is the "life of every party," telling jokes and singing solos on karaoke nights at the Moose Lodge.

Thank you, God, for my son, Richard.

CINDY

Cindy was born in Bakersfield, California, on November 21, 1952. She was a beautiful baby with blonde hair, brown eyes, and a smile to break your heart. Her grammar school days were in Garden Grove at Clinton School. She was an outstanding student and had lots of friends. She played the piano and sang in the choir. In Junior High School she won a scholarship to a voice camp at Idlewild, California.

It was at this time that Cindy changed the spelling of her name to Cindi. Her girlfriends idolized her. Her tanned skin and well-proportioned figure drew the attention of the boys. Because of her athletic ability, she still holds the record at Doig Junior High School for races and the long jump.

Even though she had accepted Jesus into her life at the age of 10, she seemed to be going in the opposite direction at this point in her life.

Her sophomore year in high school brought a real change in her life. Wayne had been elected as the representative from our church to the General Assembly in Kansas City. He was away from home for one week, and during this time I chaperoned Cindi, Debbie, Richard, and some of their friends at a beach house in Newport Beach for a week. Wow, was I crazy or what?

I had the entire Christian Women's Club board praying for me and all these kids. Some of the girls I hardly knew and had never met their parents, but we went ahead with the beach plans. We divided the group. I had Richard, Debbie, and her girlfriend with me upstairs while the remainder of the group was in the house below us, right on 15th Street in Newport.

I was very apprehensive. A couple of the girls seemed quite wild. But something wonderful happened. At dusk on the very first night we were there, the girls came running into the house. "There are some boys, they look like hippies, real cool guys. They play guitars and sing and want us to come down on the sand after dinner. They are from Calvary Chapel."

Wow. Were our prayers answered? Every evening they were entertained and preached to by these boys, and they loved it.

The leader, Rob, took a liking to Cindi and gave her his Living New Testament and encouraged her to read it, which she did.

Wayne called from Kansas City to check on us. He was extremely opposed to the hippie groups with their long hair and beads, and when I told him that the girls were spending time with this group of boys, he hit the ceiling. Cindi had convinced me Rob was a "good guy" who just "looked funny," and she wanted to date him.

She became a true believer that summer and was a changed girl. She sang hymns, read the Bible, and was happier than I had ever seen her. I liked what I saw. Even her girlfriends had changed.

Wayne was slowly convinced Rob was okay, and he reluctantly gave his permission for Cindi to date him.

The big night arrived. A knock at the door, and Cindi gleefully greeted Rob and brought him in to meet me. With his beard, long dark hair, sandals, peaceful spirit and soft brown eyes, he looked like a painting of Jesus.

His car was an old Woody with psychedelic paintings on the side. Two of the doors were missing. I was praying the neighbors weren't looking. Pride? Yes. The boy was wonderful. I just couldn't stand his looks and the crazy car, and I knew that Wayne would probably have a stroke.

Wayne *was* disturbed, but because of the change in Cindi we gradually accepted Rob.

Their relationship lasted only a few months, but Cindi continued to grow spiritually. She read the entire Bible that summer.

It was sometime after this that Cindi came home from our church and said, "Mom, Dad, do you know that blond boy in Dad's Sunday School class named Danny?"

I didn't know him, of course, but Wayne did. Danny was the track star of Bolsa Grande High School. "Yes," he said, "Nice kid. Why?"

"Well, I think he's really cute. He's Marty's brother. I'm going to get her to introduce me to him." Marty was Cindi's very good friend.

Cindi talked and giggled with Marty and all of her friends about Danny. He was dating Sharon, who was blonde and cute, but Cindi pursued him and Danny didn't seem to mind. Sharon slowly disappeared, and Danny stepped into our family. Cindi was delighted. She began seeing more and more of Danny and less of her friends. Danny was at our home almost every evening and weekend. He was tall, blond, thin, athletic, moody, and quiet. Danny and Cindi were obviously in love.

Danny greeted Cindi at the front door on her 16th birthday with a cake and a huge birthday card he had made. He was very artistic. The inside of the card had a picture of him as a child with the words, "From Danny the Kid." The cake was delicious.

We saw much of Danny over the next two years. Wayne and I could see what was happening. They were falling more and more in love, and there was absolutely nothing we could do about it. We had other plans for our daughter. We had hoped that after high school she would attend college, preferably Pasadena College because we had loved it so and because of all our experiences there. She made it very clear, however, that she wanted only one thing, to marry Danny as soon as she graduated from high school.

On the night of Cindi's graduation from high school, she ran into our bedroom about midnight with a beautiful engagement ring on her finger. Our hearts sank as she revealed her plans to be married in November on her 18th birthday. That was a sleepless night.

We did insist that Cindi train for something to help her get a job, so she enrolled in a private technical school to become a dental assistant. Within six months she had completed the course, received her diploma, and was ready to start work.

Plans were well underway for the wedding. Our budget was small and Cindi's ideas were big, so we compromised. We shopped for bargains. Cindi had expensive tastes, and many times we argued over prices. We found a beautiful, modest gown for around $80, and I made the train and the headpiece. The bridesmaids were, of course, her four best girlfriends. Debbie, her sister, was the maid of honor. I helped sew their lime green and royal blue dresses. Our son, Dickie, was a candle lighter. The entire wedding, including the dessert reception, cost about $1,800.

Cindi and Danny Spencer were married on November 21, 1970, Cindi's 18th birthday, at the First Church of the Nazarene in Long Beach, California. Approximately 300 guests attended. It was a beautiful wedding. Cindi's long, platinum-blonde hair was stunning, and her face glowed. Danny looked very tall and handsome in his tuxedo.

This was an extremely happy time for Wayne and me, but we both knew they would have many problems since they were so young. This was their choice, however, and no one could change their minds. We cherished the moments with our happy daughter and all our friends and family.

Their first small apartment was in Huntington Beach. Cindi decorated it beautifully on their meager income.

Danny worked the graveyard shift at Ralph's Supermarket, and Cindi worked in a dental office.

I went through a severe bout of depression about six months after the wedding. I thought I was going crazy. I went to several doctors and even the Oncology Clinic in Los Angeles to be tested for a brain tumor, but the doctors could find nothing. Everyone was very concerned. I stopped many of my activities, took a few hormone shots, studied as much as I could about nutrition and vitamins, and prayed a lot. In about six months, I was back to normal. It was a very weird experience. I now believe it was the onset of menopause, even though I was only 40.

On November 2, 1972, Cindi and Danny presented us with a beautiful grandson, Billy Shad. He was born in a small hospital just around the corner from our home in Santa Ana. I'll never forget Shad's birth. Cindi was in labor at our home because Danny was working. I summoned Wayne from his work, called Debbie and Dickie at their schools, and we all timed her labor pains with Wayne's stopwatch.

I was so nervous. I remember over-cleaning the house, I was so anxious. When the pains were three minutes apart, we all went to the hospital. Debbie and Dickie brought friends. I called my mother. It was quite an occasion. We called Danny, and we all awaited the arrival of our first grandchild. After three or four more hours of labor, the doctor burst through the door to announce, "You have a grandson." He allowed me to enter the delivery room, and Cindi looked up at me with glowing eyes. "Mom, I had a boy." We cried, and I leaned forward to kiss her. We rejoiced in the miracle.

ANOTHER MOVE

Even though Wayne continued to teach and coach at Los Amigos High School in Fountain Valley, he began working as a salesperson for a land-investment company. He became very successful and our income increased dramatically, which allowed me to stop teaching in our home. We moved to a beautiful, two-story townhouse on Bake Street in Westminster. Dickie was extremely disturbed about this since he was starting his junior year at Santiago High School. Debbie had already graduated from high school and had moved from our home to search for her independence. She never returned to live with us.

I had been experiencing severe back pain for quite a while and ultimately had to have back surgery to remove a ruptured disk. The surgery was successful, and I was back to playing the organ at church and playing tennis (not too strenuously!) only a few months later. It took about two years for the pain to completely subside, but I thank God for a complete healing.

Debbie was working for Marie Callender's and going to school at Orange Coast College. She also attended Brook's College in Long Beach. She was always interested in interior design and was taking courses toward this goal.

She married Bill Blanchard in Hawaii. We were not able to attend because of our financial situation and conflicting dates. We still regret that we did not attend.

She and Bill later had a reception in Huntington Beach at her in-laws. Debbie and Bill set up housekeeping in Santa Ana. Bill was in real estate and was doing well.

MOVING AGAIN!

Our lifestyle became easier. We had more vacations, better cars, and nicer clothes. This lasted about two years, and then the company went broke. All of Wayne's investors lost their investments, and we did too. We lost our home, our cars, our furniture. We kept $1,000 to put down on a very small condo. Wayne suffered a nervous breakdown and my mother passed away during this time, but God saw us through again.

We relocated to a small condo in Garden Grove on La Jolla Plaza near Brookhurst. I started teaching piano in our home again.

We celebrated our 25th wedding anniversary in the clubhouse. Our children gave us a delightful party and an inscribed silver service. Many friends attended.

Wayne gradually recuperated from this terrible emotional and financial collapse. He continued to teach and coach all during this trying time.

We were in our small condo about two years and decided to relocate to a larger place. We sold the condo, made $20,000, and bought a triple-wide mobile home. Bolsa Grande Estates on Bolsa in Westminster was our new home

We lived there for two years with our son, Dickie, and then decided to move again. We again made about $20,000 in the transaction and bought a foreclosure home in Garden Grove on Pleasant Place. It was much abused, but we could see its beauty. We moved in and started the clean-up. Perhaps this would be our retirement home, we thought. A friend remarked that we had turned a shack into a palace. My decorating courses helped me, and I really enjoyed the restoration process. I continued to teach piano. I now had a beautiful grand piano and a concert organ in our living room.

DEBBIE AND BILL'S MARRIAGE BREAKUP

Debbie and Bill were married only seven years. They had two beautiful children, Brandon and Nicole. Their backgrounds were so different that they had an extremely difficult time understanding one another. They were very unhappy in their relationship and argued much. Bill left Debbie early in her pregnancy with Nicole, two weeks before Christmas. Brandon was only a year old. We were all devastated, to say the least.

Debbie and Brandon moved in with us for about two weeks. She was afraid to be alone and was very sick from her pregnancy. We grieved together over Bill's leaving. We made the best of a very sad time.

Debbie chose to return with Brandon to her own home around Christmas. Needless to say, it was not a very happy Christmas.

Bill returned just before Nicole was born but only stayed a few months and then was gone for good. Nicole was born on May 20. Debbie and the children moved to a rental in Corona del Mar.

Debbie was left alone with two very young children. She enrolled in college, studied interior design, and started a new life. Her strength amazed us. She was single about eight years.

FAMILY FEUD

In 1981, while we were living in the mobile home, Cindi called me. "Mom, guess what I've done?"

"What, Cindi?"

"I sent our picture in to Family Feud."

"What?" I exclaimed.

"Yeah, and they want us to come up for an interview."

"Oh, Cindi, I'd be too nervous, and I'd have to kiss Richard Dawson."

"No, you won't," she said. "I bought the game and we can all get together and play it. Won't that be fun?"

Well, I conceded and decided to go along with the fun. We played the game nightly.

The first interview was such fun, and they called us back for a second interview in front of the producer. A year later they called us to come up to the studio and tape the game. It was so exciting. Debbie got 146 points on fast money, and Cindi went over the top. We came away with $10,545. It was such a happy memory with our family. I bought a new piano, and we went to Hawaii.

RICHARD AND DONNA

Our son Dickie moved from our mobile home to be on his own when he was about 23. He moved into a home with a married couple. When the couple's baby was born, the baby shared the room with Dickie! He even attended to the night feedings.

When Dickie met Donna Franks, Donna didn't like the name Dickie. So we all started calling him Richard.

Richard and Donna were married in San Diego—alone. Later a reception was held in Debbie's home for them. Donna had a young son, Curtis, who later became Richard's adopted son. They lived in Garden Grove.

LIFE MOVES ON

Our family seemed to be pulling it all together. Richard now had a stable position with Smart & Final, and Donna also had a full-time job. Debbie was single and living in Laguna Niguel. She was finishing her decorating courses at Orange Coast College and was being a mother to her two children, Brandon and Nicole.

Cindi and Danny bought an older home near us and were fixing it up. Both of them were very creative. Cindi's artistic touches turned the house into a showplace. Shad was doing well in school, winning county spelling bees and excelling in athletics. Shane was darling. He always had something cute to say, and his antics were priceless.

Wayne and I were happy with our sense of freedom and felt that all three of our children were now pretty self-sufficient. We were very thankful for that. They always worked and managed their lives well.

Wayne continued to teach at Los Amigos. I taught piano and organ in our home and began my 40th year as church organist. Christian Women's Club played a big part in my life.

Wayne became more and more active in the Master Olympics. He traveled to New York, Canada, Mexico and other parts of the world to compete in track meets. He enjoyed this very much. Many times I would accompany him on his travels. He won many medals during this time of his life.

Wayne and I were able to travel with friends more often now. We went to Canada, New England, Europe, and we both were enjoying good health. Jim and Doris Finn were with us on these trips.

Tennis was our exercise as well as our social time. We played weekly with friends and with Danny. When Debbie was married to Bill, he also played. We had some great matches. Saturday mornings were filled with breakfast and tennis with our friends. Many times they would all come to our home for lunch and swimming afterward. What fun we all had. We were in our 50s, and it was a very happy time in our lives.

Wayne and I were never church-hoppers, but we felt that our time at the Nazarene Church was finished. We decided to try a new church in Irvine recommended by some of our friends. They particularly liked the pastor, Tim Timmons.

We visited one Sunday and decided we would make the change. South Coast Community Church (SCCC) was dynamic, growing, youth-oriented and met our needs.

Our entire family made the transition. Cindi and Danny and their children changed to this church when we did. Debbie and her children also attended.

On Sunday mornings we would meet friends and family at Coco's by the airport for breakfast, and then we would fill a large section of the SCCC auditorium.

Life was good—good friends, good family relations, good health. Not just good, it was great! Our grandchildren brought us such joy. We had a comfortable home and a good steady income. It was probably the most uncomplicated time of our lives.

Arlane, 2 years old (1932)

Arlane, 10 months

Arlane, speaking

Arlane, Graduation 1948

Caption: Chuck and Arlane's Wedding, 2/22/1997

Cindi, 30 years old

Daddy, 1925

Mother, 20 years old (1923)

Nany Mama Perry

Our Family, 1958

Our Family, 1993

Wayne and Arlane

Wayne, Arlane and grandchildren

CHAPTER 9

Family Tragedy

Cindi and Danny's marriage was, as far as we could see, somewhat rocky from the beginning. Cindi wished she had not married so young. She regretted not going to college before she married. Cindi and Danny seemed to always have financial struggles, and Cindi had to work to make ends meet. She was intelligent and became bored and did not stay at any job too long.

Cindi had completed a dental-assistant program right after high school and was hired immediately by one dentist and then another. She discovered she didn't like this kind of work. She was always interested in financial work and started working for the Bank of America in various locations.

Danny was employed at Ralph's Supermarket when they were married. He worked for Ralph's for about three years and then changed to Smart & Final. He became manager of one of their markets at a very young age and continued to be employed there for about 10 years.

Their first son, Shad, was as feisty as they come with the blondest hair we had ever seen. He had a spunky nature and could run like a deer even at the age of three.

When Shad was six years old another little boy, Jeremy Shane, was born into their family. Shane, too, was beautiful. (No grandmother is ever biased!) He had blond hair and brown eyes and a cute little personality. He kept us laughing with his funny antics. He was, and still is, very athletic. His Grandpa Wayne hated that, of course!

Danny and Cindi spent much time with their boys. They were involved with school projects and programs. They were constantly at Shad's Little League football games. They were active at the Nazarene Church in Long Beach and later attended South Coast Community in Irvine. Many of their weekends were spent with Wayne and me. We had family picnics and barbeques at the beach. We vacationed with them in Palm Springs and spent a week with them in Hawaii.

Even though there was discord in their marriage, they displayed a rather happy family life. Cindi seldom spoke of her discontentment with Danny, but we could see her unhappiness in the things she said to him. She and I would talk sometimes and she would just sigh and say, "Well I guess I can't do anything about it, so I'll just stick it out."

During this time Cindi took some courses at church on marriage. She read books. They both attended a marriage seminar. They were attending church regularly, but the marriage seemed to be gradually disintegrating. Cindi seemed to be growing more and unhappy.

Danny could feel her pulling away, and he began to tighten the reins. The more he tightened, the more she pulled away until a real tug-of-war began. Their quarreling was continuous. A counselor suggested they separate for a while, so they decided to do just that.

When they first separated, Danny slept in his van in the parking lot at work. The neighborhood was quite rough, so his best friend loaned him a gun for his protection. I asked Cindi if that scared her. She replied, "Nope, he's just trying to make me think he's going to shoot himself," and laughed.

Danny moved in with good friends. Cindi stayed with the boys in their home on Geraldine Street in Garden Grove. Everyone was in turmoil. Wayne and I were extremely distressed and anxious.

The place where Danny was staying was loud and confusing. He called to see if he and Shad could stay in our guest bedroom for a few days until their house in Newport was ready. Of course we agreed, and they moved in that evening.

Danny and Shad stayed with us, and Cindi and Shane stayed in their home. We were in contact with her. Danny seemed better. Having Shad with him lifted his spirits. They were with us only three or four days. During this time, Cindi became extremely depressed. I'm sure she was questioning her decision.

Days were heavy. We called Cindi daily. One evening she called us hysterically, wanting us to come over and just be with her. We entered the darkened house. She was curled up in a fetal position on the couch in the family room, sobbing as if her heart would break. Shane was near her on the floor playing. We tried to comfort her. She spoke through her sobs, "I don't know whether I'm doing the right thing, Mom and Dad." We just held her and prayed quietly. She was so torn up and frustrated, and we were too. As parents we wanted her to be happy and knew that she was not happy like this. We told her it was her choice and only she knew her own heart and circumstances. I wondered if she really did.

I looked around the almost empty room. Their house was sold and was going through escrow. Many things had been packed. The pictures, dishes, and beautiful knickknacks they had carefully selected during their 13 years of marriage seemed to mean nothing now. The television was on, but no one was watching it. There was such a feeling of emptiness and sadness as we talked.

Wayne and I decided to get them out of the house and to go to Debbie's in Laguna Niguel. Wayne hid his feelings with some light talk, and we spent the rest of the evening talking over things with Debbie.

Debbie invited Cindi and Shane to move in with her. Shad was going to live with his father in an apartment in Newport Beach.

Because Cindi was so upset, we suggested that Danny and Shad move back to the empty house and that Cindi and Shane come to our house. They did, but only for a few days. Cindi was in constant contact with her sister, Debbie, and was doing much better emotionally.

Things were settling down. Danny seemed to be reconciled to the separation. He loved having Shad with him. He had even bought Shad a new wetsuit and surf-board, getting ready for their beach house. They had checked out the new school, right on the sand at Newport. Wayne and I were very apprehensive about this arrange-ment but said nothing about the decision.

It was Wednesday, March 7, 1984. I was teaching in our living room, and the door opened. There stood Cindi and Shane, grinning. "Mom, everything is going to be okay. Don't worry."

I looked up with relief. I had not seen her smile for quite some time. She went on to explain that she and Shane had completed their move into Debbie's house. She said, "I'll be by the house tomorrow to clean and maybe stop by for lunch, if you'll be home. I was usually home, so of course I agreed. I was happy to see her seem-ingly peaceful once again. I said goodbye to them and continued with my teaching.

That evening Danny and Shad came for dinner. After dinner Danny started to help me clean the table, while Wayne and Shad retired to the family room to watch a ballgame.

Danny seemed unusually disturbed. He explained he had not eaten or slept well for three weeks and had lost 25 pounds. He began to cry, telling me again of his mis-ery. We stood in the kitchen, crying and talking. He was deeply hurt. I could see the agony in his eyes as he wept and talked.

I tried to comfort him. We prayed and talked more. He felt he could not handle the separation. He could not let Cindi go.

I tried to explain that perhaps only a few months of separation would bring her back again, but he could not see this. He kept crying. We hugged each other. I quoted Scripture about peace and comfort. We turned to John 14:27 and read together, *"Peace I leave with you, My peace I give to you; not as the world gives do I give to you. Let not your heart be troubled, neither let it be afraid."* I reminded him that Jesus said, *"I will never leave you or forsake you"* (Hebrews 13:5). God will bring us through anything. The evening dragged on. Finally he seemed to get a hold of himself. He dried his eyes, called to Shane, backed down the steps and said goodbye for the evening.

On March 8, 1984, I awoke to a beautiful spring morning. The sun was pouring into our bedroom. I could hear the baby birds near the window. I was anticipating a brighter day.

As usual, after breakfast I took my place at the piano and waited for my first piano student.

The day progressed well. I greeted each student cheerfully and was looking forward to noon when I would see Cindi for lunch.

Twelve o'clock came, no Cindi. I waited. Then 12:30 p.m., no Cindi. I ate by myself and resumed my lessons at 1:00 p.m. I was terribly disappointed, but I knew she had much to do and probably had decided to work through lunch.

Around 2:15 p.m., the door opened. It was Shad. I was delighted to see him. He told me his dad had instructed him to come straight from school to our house. His dad would pick him up about 2:30 p.m. to attend his grandpa's track meet.

"I'm so excited, Grandma, I get to time the track meet. I can hardly wait! It is the biggest track meet of the year, you know."

I asked him to go into the family room and wait while I continued with the piano lessons.

As each lesson would come, Shad would run to the door, expecting to see his dad, only to let another child in for me. I suggested that he call his dad's work. "Perhaps he has been delayed." Danny was rarely late, and he would always call to let us know. Shad called his dad's work and they told him, "He left work at 1:00 p.m."

We were both quite anxious by this time. Shad again went back to the family room to wait for his father.

Three o'clock came. No Danny. Then 3:30 p.m., no Danny. Four o'clock and 4:15 p.m. passed. At approximately 4:30 p.m., the doorbell rang. I excused myself from the girl who was seated at the piano and opened the door. Two policemen were standing on the front porch.

My heart was pounding. "Is something wrong?" I asked, trembling.

The one on the left showed me his badge and solemnly said, "There has been a shooting."

"Who has been shot?" I gasped, recalling the gun that Danny had been given by his best friend for protection.

"Your daughter has been shot," he replied.

"How bad is she?" I inquired.

"She's dead." Both policemen stood silently with lowered eyes.

I could only whisper, "My daughter is dead," over and over again.

The policeman on the right spoke. "And Danny has shot himself."

"Oh, no," I gasped, "Is he dead, too?"

"No, but he is paralyzed. The bullet is stuck in his spine just behind his heart. He evidently tried to kill himself."

Silence. The piano stopped. The air was still. My first thought was of God. Where was He? What do I do now? Pray. Yes, I must pray. Help, God, I need help. Help me, help me. Please. Right now. I need you. Please give me strength to go through this. Please give me Your peace. Jesus, God, I really need you. You told me you would never leave me or forsake me. You said you would comfort me and be my help in the time of trouble. In my darkest hour, Lord, I need you. PLEASE HELP ME."

I began to recall all the songs I had sung and played on the piano during my childhood. "Peace, Peace, Wonderful Peace Coming Down from the Father Above," and many others. Bible memory verses I had learned through the years began to flood my mind. *"Trust in the Lord with all of your heart and lean not on your own understanding. In all your ways acknowledge Him and He will direct your path"* (Proverbs 3:5–6).

I could not understand what was happening. I only knew I trusted God, and somehow He had allowed this to happen to our family.

I prayed and waited. No tears. No screams. Just silence. I was waiting for my God to rescue me. The two policemen stood in silence. I looked toward heaven as if to be taken up. Five, ten minutes passed. Then, like an invisible comforter sweeping around me softly, so softly, His peace came. I was lifted. I felt light as a feather. I looked at the two men. They just stared at me. I smiled. "God has given me peace and strength right now."

A picture of Danny appeared before me, a young man we had loved since he was 17, so disturbed and frustrated. I still loved him. And then I saw a line drawn and the horrible crime that he had committed and absolutely hated that. He had killed our daughter. Loved him/hated the crime. It was so clear to me, and to this day I still have the same feeling.

We walked into the living room. One officer dismissed the piano student. She looked at me with agony in her eyes. Our two sofas were at the upholsterer's shop, and we had nothing to sit on. The young men knelt beside me while I lay on my side on the carpet.

I quickly gathered my thoughts. "Who shall I call first?"

"Your husband."

"I can't. He's on a track field somewhere."

"Family, pastor, friends," they suggested.

I walked toward the telephone in the kitchen. One by one I dialed people, relating the tragic news. All were stunned and said they would come immediately.

I'll never forget the calls to my other two children. I called Debbie first and told her in one sentence what had happened. She screamed and screamed. Her children started screaming. I tried to calm her but could not. I suggested she call a close friend to be with her. I asked her to come to our house as soon as possible. She calmed down somewhat.

While I was talking to Debbie, Shad peeked his head around the corner. "What's the matter, Grandma?" I immediately took him to the den, sat down on the couch and tearfully explained, "Your dad has shot and killed your mother, and your dad has shot himself. He is not dead, but he is in the hospital."

Shad cried, "Why? Why did he do that?"

We had a hard time trying to console each other. I tried to help him by saying, "Many people have lived with no mothers, Shad."

He replied, "Abraham Lincoln did."

"Yes," I wept, "Your mother is in heaven now with Jesus, Shad. Someday we will all be together."

Arm in arm we left the den, took our places in the living room, and just sat there thinking.

One of the policemen asked me the whereabouts of Shane. I told him Shane was at a preschool and gave him the location. He left to go pick him up.

Then I called my son, Richard. I did not tell him over the phone what had happened. I just couldn't. I only said, "Hi, what are you doing? Are you through eating? Could you all come over as soon as possible? I have something I need to tell you."

Richard said, "Sure, Mom, we'll be right there."

The policeman returned with Shane, who had just turned five years old. He jumped into my arms and hugged me. I told him what had happened. He just kept hugging me.

Next on the list was our pastor, Tim Timmons. Then, as people were beginning to gather in our home, the phone rang. It was Wayne. I ran to the bedroom to answer it.

"Hi, Hon, we won the track meet, the upset of the season." I could hear the excitement in his voice.

I broke in, "Wayne, Wayne, I need you home with me right now."

"I can't. The bus isn't here for the team, and I have to stay until the last boy leaves."

"Wayne, please come home now. Danny has shot and killed Cindi." There, it was out. I couldn't hold it in any longer.

There was silence, then a blood-curdling yell. "No, no, it can't be. No, I can't believe it. I'll be right there."

Wayne arrived sobbing, nearly fainting. We held each other, crying and shaking in our grief. Why? Why? It was so unnecessary.

Our crying subsided as friends, relatives and our pastor entered our home. Each hugged us and wept, sharing our grief. Our dear friends Jim and Doris Finn, Paul and Connie Montgomery, Jan and Bill Bogard, and Bill and Sondra Fry were a tremendous support at this time and for months later.

Shad and Shane stayed very close to me, Shane on my lap and Shad sitting to my side. Wayne sat on the other side. There was much crying. People shook their heads in disbelief.

Richard heard the news in the driveway. He was so angry that he kicked in the side of his car. Debbie came in crying so hard. We were all in shock.

I felt for Wayne, who had lost a daughter. I felt for Debbie and Richard, who had lost a sister. But most of all, I felt for two little boys. What was going to happen to them? I knew what I wanted to do, but what about Wayne? Did he have my same desires? Were we too old to take on children again? I was 53, and Wayne was 58. How would our lifestyle change? Would our health and finances permit this transition? How would it affect our other grandchildren?

Later I found out that the same thoughts were going through Wayne's mind. When he broke the silence with, "What about the boys?" we both said in unison, "WE WILL KEEP THEM!" There was no doubt in either of our minds. We loved them so much and could not bear the thought of releasing them to anyone else. So that was settled.

A NEW FAMILY

We moved the boys into our spare bedroom. Their bunk beds and belongings seemed to take over our home. The many cards, telephone calls, letters, flowers, food bags and other gifts poured into our home. The boys seemed quite contented. Little toy soldiers were all over the house. A bird named Elliott came to live with us. Amid the sadness of losing our daughter and our son-in-law, there was God's peace. God's Word was our source of strength and sanity. The Psalms were so comforting. A verse that we read over and over was, *"Day by day the Lord pours out His love upon me and through the night He gives me PEACE."* Neither Wayne nor I had to take any medication for sleep, nor did the boys. One afternoon Shane and I drove into our driveway. I burst into tears as I laid my head on the steering wheel, sobbing as if my heart would break.

Shane leaned over, put his hand on my arm and said, "What's the matter, Grandma?"

I replied, "Oh Shane, I miss your mother so much."

Shane looked at me and said, "Grandma, aren't we glad that God is in control of everything?"

I lifted my head, dried my tears, and gave him a big kiss.

Approximately six weeks after the tragedy, the phone rang and a very weak voice said, "I'm so sorry." It was Danny.

I called Wayne and the boys to join me. We were all trembling.

He sobbed, "I'm so sorry. I'm so sorry."

I broke into his words. "We love you, Danny, and we forgive you."

We all cried. One by one we talked to him, telling him we still loved him and forgave him. Only God could do this for us.

Danny was no longer paralyzed, but the bullet was still lodged in his spine causing him digestion difficulties. He spent one and a half years in the Orange County Jail and was then transferred to Northern California for a short time before being sent to Chino Minimum Security Prison for Men for two years. We visited him occasionally with the boys. He began to look better and was healing emotionally. One afternoon as we were leaving Chino, Shane, who was seated beside me in the back seat, remarked, "GRANDMA, IS THIS REAL LIFE?" I answered, "This is real life, but God helps us every day, doesn't he?"

Our lives began to change. Wayne continued to teach but would arrive home earlier to help me with the boys. I took on more piano students because of the added expenses. Debbie and Richard visited frequently, helping in any way they could. We put our home up for sale and decided to move to Irvine, California, where we could have a fresh start with the boys.

Wayne pursued all the legal matters regarding the custody of Shad and Shane, and by September we had sold our home and purchased a two-story home on Royale in Irvine. It was a wonderful home. We paid $165,000 for it. It had four bedrooms and a large family room. It was a welcomed change. No longer did we have to frequently pass the street where Cindi and Danny and the boys had lived or eat in restaurants where we had memories of meeting them for breakfast or pass the bank where Cindi had been employed. We did what we could to be free of those painful memories.

Across the street from our new home was a small neighborhood park where the boys could play safely, and their school was within walking distance. Woodbridge Lake was nearby also. Shane and I spent many hours relaxing on the banks and fishing. Everything in Irvine was clean and green and fresh.

A new routine began. Shane was in kindergarten now, and I made arrangements for him to be picked up after school by the Young Sportsmen's Club until I could return for him after my day's work at a music studio in Laguna Niguel. Shad was enrolled in the fifth grade at Los Neranjos School, only five blocks from our home.

Both of the boys loved athletics, which they excelled in, and kept us extremely busy transporting them to their practices and games. Soccer, baseball, and football were their favorite sports. Our home was alive with laughter, cooking, friends, and animals. We had fish, a lizard, a white rat, a new kitty named "Maui," and a bird named "Elliott." Wayne and I were active in the PTA. I became a room mother again!

One morning I prayed, "God, please give me the patience that I need to raise these two little boys. Please give me the physical strength of a 30-year-old. Please give me the mental capacity of a 30-year-old and the body of a 30-year-old." I chuckled, and I know He did too. That evening at the grocery store, Shad called to me, "Grandma, can I get some of this gum?" The clerk looked at me and remarked, "Are *you* his grandmother?" I just silently said a sentence prayer, "Thank you, God! You've already answered one of my prayers." Those were very happy days.

Our home was bouncing with new friends. Shad brought his classmates home daily. There was David, who was taking chemotherapy for bone cancer, and Bryan, who became a permanent part of our family. Shad's secret room behind his closet in his bedroom became a haven for his friends. He had fixed it up with little benches and a table. No one was allowed in there except these special boys. Secrets were shared, and after I found not-so-appropriate magazines, I had to put a halt to those meetings.

Shane and I spent many good times together. One fishing trip to Woodbridge Lake turned out to be quite interesting. We prepared a lunch, I took a book, and Shane took all of his fishing gear. I drove to the lake, settled down on the grass with my book and lunch. It was only moments before I heard Shane shriek, "Grandma, I've caught a fish." I jumped up from the grass and grabbed the pole only to find one big, ugly catfish on his hook. I yelled, "Shane, put it back in the water." We swung the pole up and down, but the fish was ours and I had no clue how to take that hook out of his mouth. I emptied the sandwiches out of the plastic bag, filled it with water and rushed the fish and the attached pole to the car. I hurriedly drove home.

Our housekeeper, Mary, was there and rescued us, cutting the hook from the fish's mouth and dropping the fish into a large tub that we had in the garage. The following morning we found the fish floating lifeless in the water. Shane and I were disappointed, but we had shared a very exciting experience.

The table that once held flowers and crystal now displayed a fish tank and lots of little bug jars. Shane brought home a bag full of crickets one day to feed his lizards and he forgot to clip the opening, so that night all of the crickets escaped all over our two-story home. It was about two years before we got all of them. Our home sounded like a wilderness for months to come.

One evening in September I was engaged to play the organ for a wedding in Newport. It was getting cold and foggy around 5:00 p.m., and I was supposed to be at the church at 6:30 p.m. I called for Shane. No Shane. Wayne and Shad were in Garden Grove for football practice. I became very nervous, as it was getting dark, and called

911. The police came immediately. They searched our home and pool area first, and then they sent four or five policemen into the neighborhood, quizzing all the people. No Shane. I was petrified. Where was he?

Two hours passed. Then, through teary eyes, I barely made out a boy's figure on a bicycle heading toward our house. He stopped in front of me. It was Shane. "Grandma, why are all of the police cars here?" he asked.

"They are looking for you. Where have you been?"

"I've been at Dusty's house, my new friend."

I scolded him, dismissed the amused policemen and then hugged him, crying my eyes out, so thankful he was safe.

I loved going on field trips with Shane and his class. All the children called me "Grandma." Sea World was my favorite. I was in charge of seven very lively boys and occasionally lost two or three, but we all returned safely.

Our new family attended South Coast Community Church in Irvine, where Tim Timmons was the pastor, every Sunday and sometimes during the week. Shad was involved in the youth programs. Debbie and our grandchildren, Brandon and Nicole, also attended, and many Sundays we would all have lunch out or at our home.

We also hosted a weekly Bible study in our home. About 20 people attended every Thursday evening to study the Bible and to fellowship. Wayne was the leader, and Shane and I prepared the food. Shane loved it when we had potlucks.

Two Wonderful Gifts from God

On Mother's Day, 1984, just two months after Cindi's death, I was looking through some of her treasures. I picked up her childhood Bible and began to leaf through it. On one of the front pages was written in her handwriting these precious words: *"Today I invited Jesus Christ into my heart. When I die I will live with Him in Heaven forever."* She was ten years old at the time this was written.

What a wonderful Mother's Day gift from God!

God gave me another gift through Wayne's sister, Juanita. She was in a coma in the hospital, suffering from emphysema. Wayne and I walked into her hospital room to be with her during her last moments on earth. We stood above her weeping as we prayed for her.

She suddenly opened her eyes and whispered, "I just saw Cindi."

"You did? What did she look like?"

Juanita, who was barely breathing, said, "She was BEAUTIFUL!"

"Did she say anything to you, Juanita?' I waited and waited for her answer.

She mouthed these words, "Cindi held out her arms to me and said, "I WILL HELP YOU OVER."

Juanita breathed a deep sigh and peacefully passed away.

Cindi, someday we will all be with you. We want you to help us over too. Until then, we will cherish your memory."

Thank you, dear God, for these two wonderful gifts!

THE TRIAL

I was awakened by the shrill ring of the telephone on a rainy day in December 1984. The voice on the other end was the district attorney informing our family that the trial for Danny Franklin Spencer would begin on December 13, 1984. A jury of 12 men and women had been carefully selected. Wayne and I, our daughter Debbie and possibly Shad, just 12 years old, would be summoned to appear on the witness stand. Although we had been expecting this, we were really not ready for the agonizing time ahead of us.

Danny's attorney, Jim Riddett of Santa Ana, a kind and gracious gentleman in his early 40s, was in constant contact with us during the next few weeks.

On December 13, 1984, Room 212 of the Santa Ana court house was filled with inquisitive onlookers, newspaper reporters, a high school civics class, friends, relatives, guards, the jury, attorneys, and the judge. Witnesses were not allowed in the court room until they were summoned to the witness stand.

Day after day, witness after witness, the trial dragged on. Danny entered the courtroom daily in handcuffs and chains with guards on either side of him. He was extremely thin and gaunt. He looked so sad, so anxious.

Christmas vacation interrupted the procedure. The trial was postponed until January.

The trial resumed with the questioning of witnesses day after day. Wayne and I were still waiting to be called to the stand. Finally the words pierced the silence of the courthouse corridor, "Mrs. Arlane Ambrose, to the witness stand please."

What does one say when she must tell all she knows about a son-in-law of 13 years, a friend for 17 years, the father of her two grandsons? The truth. Questions were fired at me, and the jury's eyes were all glued to mine. As I unfolded my story, Danny laid his head on his arms and wept. The jury all cried with me as I told of my love for my daughter and my concern for my son-in-law. Emotion was too high, and I could not go on. The trial was discontinued until the next day.

The following morning brought renewed strength. As I was ushered to the witness stand, I quietly asked the guard to please remove the gun that was used in the crime and Cindi's clothes from my sight. I again prayed for strength from Almighty God. I prayed for a sharp mind, a clear memory and good communication with the attorneys.

Danny walked into the courtroom. He smiled slightly, almost as if he knew I still loved him. I knew in my heart that only God could give me that kind of love for him.

I was very calm this day as I relived many incidents prior to March 8, 1984, and explained in detail his relationships with our daughter, our grandsons, and our family. The district attorney was stunned by my answers. He shook his head in disgust, not believing that the mother-in-law of a murderer could have that kind of compassion. I was on the witness stand for five hours.

My husband, Wayne, also testified for Danny. They were extremely close friends. I was not allowed to hear his testimony, but I know that Wayne also was not bitter and had forgiven Danny. Our daughter, Debbie, gave a similar testimony.

Shad was interviewed at our home in Irvine by the district attorney and Mr. Ridditt. They both decided it was pertinent to the case that he appear in court. I was unhappy over their decision. We came to an agreement that the jury would not be present during Shad's testimony. I sat beside him with a glass of water, and my hand on his arm. He answered all of the questions with little emotion.

The audience was puzzled by our reactions. The jury was undecided. The judge, a most kind gentleman, was bewildered. The attorneys continued their questioning. Many days passed. March rolled around, and the decision of the jury was upon us now. The jury could not decide, so the judge began to speak.

Day 1—Judge: "I want to help you come to a decision. Vote on whether Danny Spencer should be convicted of first degree murder."

Hours passed. Everyone was tense. The jury returned to the courtroom. "NOT GUILTY of first-degree murder!"

Shouts could be heard. Danny's family wept audibly.

Day 2—Judge: "Now, I want you to decide if Danny Spencer is guilty of second degree murder."

Hours passed so slowly. The courtroom was extremely tense.

The jury returned. "NOT GUILTY of second degree murder."

The courtroom was buzzing.

Day 3—Judge: "Now, would you please decide if Danny Spencer is guilty of manslaughter."

Many hours passed. The courtroom was extremely quiet at this time. Two and a half hours later, the jury entered the courtroom and explained that they could not reach a decision.

HUNG JURY ON MANSLAUGHTER

On Monday, March 2, 1985, the judge and two attorneys began to plea bargain. Danny Franklin Spencer was convicted of manslaughter with a five-year prison sentence. He had already spent one and a half years in the county jail and was given six months off for good behavior. That left only three years to serve.

Danny transferred to Chino State Minimum Security Prison for Men and was trained as a firefighter.

Following the trial he put on 25 pounds. His countenance was happy and peaceful. His faith in God matured and became strong. God was restoring his mind, body, and spirit.

The boys, Wayne and I saw him occasionally. Our visits were cheerful. We talked and laughed and looked forward to his beginning a new life.

"God is able to do exceedingly above all that we ask or think" (Ephesians 3:20).

CHAPTER 10

An Unusual Christmas

Three years after sentencing, about two weeks before Christmas, Danny was released from Chino. The boys waited anxiously for their father at the curb. He slowly and shyly walked up to our door with the boys. He looked as if he were about to burst into tears. Wayne and I met him and the boys in our front hallway, taking him through our home, room by room. His and Cindi's furniture was all through our home—the oak hutch, coffee table and other pieces. Several pictures on the walls were theirs.

At the top of the staircase was a large oil painting of Cindi. Danny stood before it in silence as he fought back his tears. It was a very emotional moment for all of us.

He stayed and talked with the boys, hugging them and telling them he wanted to do many things with them in the near future.

He spent Christmas with us. Richard and his family were with us as well as Debbie and her children. It was not the best Christmas we had ever celebrated together. Cindi's absence was very evident.

Danny was at our home almost daily until he began working in January. He wanted to be with the boys every night. He helped with the cooking and the boys' homework. He moved into an upstairs bedroom. We needed the help. Wayne's health was failing, and I was getting older and more tired. We welcomed his help with the boys. God continued to provide strength and guidance.

CHAPTER 11

Wayne's Health

Two years passed by very quickly as we cared for the boys. I taught piano and organ in our home daily. Life was settling down once again. The memory of Cindi was uppermost in our minds, but God truly gave us peace and strength to get through each day.

Wayne had been away, competing in a Master Olympics track meet in New Orleans. The door opened (I was teaching in the living room) and Wayne slowly fell onto the sofa, whispering, "Something is wrong with me. I need to see a doctor. I feel so weak, like I have the flu or something."

Wayne was never ill. He always prided himself in having such great health.

He did go to the doctor the following day and was subsequently sent to a urologist for testing and a prostate gland biopsy.

A week later, as I was teaching at the music store, the phone rang. It was Wayne. "Hi, honey. What's up?"

Wayne answered, "What are you doing at 5:30 this afternoon?"

"The boys are having haircuts. Please don't ask me to change. You know how hard it is to get in with Sherrie."

Wayne paused. "Arlane, Dr. Dicus called and wants us in his office at 5:30."

"Why?" I asked softly.

"I have prostate cancer."

"I'll be there at 5:30."

The boys were notified, and a babysitter arrived at our home. I raced to the doctor's office and met Wayne in the parking lot. We hugged and cried as we clung to each other.

How could this be? Wayne had never smoked or touched alcohol. He always ate a healthy diet and ran three to five miles daily. There was no cancer in his family's history. Neither of us could believe this news.

Dr. Dicus relieved our fears by telling us that since Wayne was so healthy, he believed the cancer was totally confined to the prostate gland. He would perform surgery to remove the gland and believed that would take care of the problem. Just to be sure, however, he would do further tests immediately and would have the results in just a few days.

We had already planned a vacation in Hawaii with the boys and our daughter, Debbie, and our grandchildren, Brandon and Nicole. Dr. Dicus advised us to go and to enjoy ourselves.

We did go, but our vacation was clouded by the devastating news. The children were unaware of the seriousness of their grandpa's condition, and they all thoroughly enjoyed our time in Hawaii.

When we returned, Dr. Dicus's office called and again requested that we meet with him on Wednesday at 5:30 p.m. With much anxiety in our hearts we went to hear the results of Wayne's medical tests.

Dr. Dicus leaned back in his chair. "Wayne, I'm so sorry. The cancer has spread to your lymph glands and there is a touch in the spine."

The news jolted us. We sat in silence.

"What shall I do now?" Wayne inquired.

"Get your matters in order," the doctor replied.

Wayne was given six months to two years to live. The cancer was quite advanced. It was in Stage 7.

Wayne wanted a second opinion. He requested that all his tests be sent to UCLA for observation. The results were the same. The doctors there directed him to receive 36 radiation treatments, which he did.

His cancer was in remission for about two years, and he felt quite normal. He again reunited with his track buddies for competition in the Master Olympics. Then the cancer reappeared.

I began to feel the stress of raising the boys and dealing with the prognosis of Wayne's cancer, even though he was leading a normal life. I was fearful and anxious. I was experiencing chest pains, and many times I felt as if I would pass out.

One morning I awoke to these symptoms and began to cry out to God for help. I screamed at Satan to leave me alone and, in the name of Jesus, rebuked the devil. I made my way to the bathroom to prepare myself for the day. As I looked into the mirror I saw dark clouds floating on the surface, but then darts started to pierce the clouds of fear and worry. They all began to disappear as the weapons of God shattered them, and they totally disintegrated. *"Greater is He that is in me than he that is in the world"* (1 John 4:4). I praised God for the healing. My depression totally disappeared.

We heard about a new alternative treatment for cancer in Quebec, Canada. We immediately boarded a plane and flew to the hospital there to start the treatment of Flutimide and Luperon (hormones), which arrested the cancer for another two years. We were so thankful for his extended life. Then the cancer returned again.

Treatment in Mexico was our next move. These treatments were quite expensive ($250 a day), but they worked. Wayne drove to Mexico daily. He stayed until the treatments were over and then returned to work. He kept this treatment going until his life ended on April 22, 1994.

During the last days and weeks, Richard spent the night at our house to help lift his father and to be with him. They became very close.

God had blessed Wayne with eight extra years of productive life. We were so grateful.

CHAPTER 12

Conclusion

"I am recording this so that future generations will also praise the Lord for ALL that He has done" (Psalm 102:18).

When Wayne was diagnosed with prostate cancer, he was given the opportunity to retire from the school system after 37 years of teaching. He was given one year of full pay, since he had never used sick leave, and lifetime retirement benefits. We decided to downsize our home and bought a condo in the Deerfield area of Irvine. Danny rented the condo next door to us. The boys were responsible to me in the daytime and to Danny at night. We jointly took care of them.

Shane and his cousin Brandon were best friends. They had great times together. One afternoon they decided to make chocolate pudding. I thought Debbie was watching them, and she thought I was watching them. They crawled into my kitchen window and proceeded to whip a pudding mix with milk. Needless to say, the entire kitchen was splattered with chocolate pudding—walls, curtains and cupboards. The boys were nowhere to be found when I arrived home!

While we were living in this condo, Debbie married Dennis Newell, who had an 11-year-old daughter, Kim. Dennis was in the development business, and Debbie's business as an interior designer was expanding. They designed and built a beautiful home on Amapola Street in Orange Park Acres. Jacquelyn and Terra were born only 15 months apart.

Wayne joined Dennis in the real estate business. Wayne did well financially, and we decided to buy a retirement home in Tustin at 12791 Brittany Woods Drive. Dennis and Wayne worked together for about five years and had a wonderful friendship.

Meanwhile, Danny met a young lady at South Coast Community Church. They fell in love and were married. Danny wanted the boys to live with them.

We agreed, but Shad returned to us after about three months while Shane stayed with them. Wayne and Shad grew even closer because Shad was playing football and running track. Wayne was at nearly all of his practices, meets and games. They were the closest of friends.

Many meals at our home were with Shad's friends, and we loved it.

We hardly saw Shane since Danny and his wife had moved to Orange. Shane was also very active in sports, and this kept him busy.

The building business waned as the nation's economy began to collapse. Wayne cashed in his life insurance to pay for medical treatments in Mexico and borrowed all of the equity in our home to invest in Newell Development. The economy continued to decline, and our income followed suit. Once again we were living on Wayne's retirement income and my piano lessons.

Wayne's health was failing, but he and Dennis decided to start the Los Angeles International Marketplace. It was a huge, upbeat swap meet in Irwindale, California. Dennis was the manager, and Wayne was in charge of selecting and working with 600 vendors. It took two years to get it started, but the Marketplace collapsed only a few months after it opened.

The tremendous stress of working 10 to 12 hours a day, seven days a week, took its toll on Wayne's health. He was no longer able to leave the house and was extremely ill. His weight dropped to 65 pounds, and he was on heavy doses of morphine to endure the pain.

On April 22, 1994, a great man left this world to be with his Creator. He had faithfully served his God since he was a teenager and was influential in leading many people to Christ.

THE EMPTY NEST AGAIN

Shad moved from our home during Wayne's illness. He was 21 years old. He chose a good friend, Bryan, to share a small apartment in Irvine. Shad idolized Wayne and had wanted him to be his Best Man when he married. The death of his grandpa devastated him.

TRANSITION

Three years of widowhood brought fear, loneliness and sadness along with new friends. I learned how to be more independent and began to enjoy the freedom of coming and going as I pleased. To help with expenses, I rented out a room in my home.

My children and grandchildren were dear to me. Richard came over in an instant to repair things or to help with heavy household chores. He installed motion-sensor lights on the outside of the house. Cats and possums triggered the lights and scared me in the middle of the night. Whenever I needed him, he was there.

Debbie was a darling. She and her family routinely had me for over for dinner and took me with her and the children to go shopping, to movies, or out to eat. She checked on me daily.

The grandchildren brought me much happiness with their cute ways and loving dispositions. Shad was very protective of me. Their love was especially comforting during this time.

God has truly blessed me with a wonderful family.

"For I know the plans I have for you, says the Lord. They are plans for good and not for evil, to give you a future and a hope" (Jeremiah 29:11).

God sent me a wonderful, godly housemate named Judy. Her voice on the phone sounded like an angel. When she came to the house to be interviewed, I knew God had sent her to me. Her wonderful Christian spirit was so evident, and she moved in that day. We had great fellowship during her stay with me until she moved to San Clemente to work for The JESUS Film Project.

Colleen was my next housemate. She was a dear and a great companion also. We laughed and cried together and got along so well.

During this period of my life, my music students increased. I started attending the Crystal Cathedral and became one of their pianists. I had many speaking engagements and met many new friends. My emotions began to heal. I became involved with single ladies in a Bible study and attended a Friday night Bible study with single adults. Single retreats led me to new friends and activities.

God has blessed me with good health, but during this time I needed to have cataracts removed from both eyes. There were complications, but God was faithful. My dear tennis friend, Pat Edwards, took me to the symphony and opera at the performing arts in Costa Mesa almost weekly. She introduced me to a wonderful organization called P.E.O, and I later joined this great group of ladies.

BRANCHING OUT

Attending services at the Crystal Cathedral was enjoyable. I loved the positive atmosphere that permeated the beautiful campus, the new friends that I made, and the teachings of Dr. Robert Schuler. Everything about my experience there was beneficial and uplifting.

When they learned I played the piano, I was asked to play for many of the Women's Ministry functions as well as the Single's ministry. My new women acquaintances were invigorating, and I enjoyed all of the activities. Norma Roberts became a very special friend at this time, as did June McBirnie.

Christian Women's Club luncheons kept me very busy. I still functioned as Area Representative for the Tustin Club and also went from club to club giving my testimony while I sang and played the piano. Connie Montgomery traveled with me much of the time.

During the summer of 1995, I accepted a speaking engagement in Lancaster, Pennsylvania. En route to Pennsylvania, I visited relatives in Fulton, Missouri, and then met Norma Roberts and Betty Price at the Philadelphia airport. Norma and Betty accompanied me for the rest of the trip. We stayed with Marian and Noah Kreider in Manheim. Our two weeks in Pennsylvania were quite an experience. The Kreiders treated us like royalty.

GAS PUMP STORY

About a year into my "single again" life and shortly after I returned from Pennsylvania, I decided to completely change my image. A new hairdo was on the list, and a few new items were added to my wardrobe.

The day that I had my hair styled in a wonderful new look, I stopped by a service station to get gasoline. Wayne had always taken care of the cars. This was just not my thing!

I felt so chic this day as I pranced around to the gas pump, pulled out the hose and nozzle, and pushed it into my tank. As I was standing at the rear of my car a truck came behind me, and the man inside waved at me. I was terribly embarrassed because I thought he was flirting with me! This new hairdo was certainly attracting attention! I smiled and waved back. I ducked my head and continued with my job. He waved again. He really does desire my attention, I thought. I smiled and waved back. Finally, the third time he not only waved but honked his horn.

He leaned out the door of his car saying with a very loud voice, "Lady, will you please close your car door? I need to get to the gas pump."

I was terribly embarrassed. It wasn't my hair after all! Because of my nervousness I quickly returned to my place in the driver's seat, started the motor, and quickly took off in a flash!

The next thing that I heard was, "LADY, LADY! STOP! LADY, STOP!"

Four men were yelling and running after me as fast as they could. I had never in my life had so much attention! I heard a clucking noise outside of the car and looked in my rear view mirror. To my horror the hose was being dragged behind my car with the nozzle still in my gas tank. The men finally caught me to retrieve their equipment, and I saw them running with it back to the station to connect it with the main gas tank.

I sped from that station, passing the man in the truck. He was rolling his eyes and shaking his head as if to say, "Just another dumb blonde."

I have never gone near that station again, and I don't know if I paid for the gasoline that day. This is just one of many crazy moments that followed my husband's absence.

NEW HUSBAND, CHUCK

During this time of my life, I dated a few men, but none appealed to me. I much preferred socializing with my lady friends. There was one man, however, I felt attracted to—Chuck Hart. Chuck had lost his wife, Bunny, nine months after Wayne had passed away. We had been friends since college days and our families had gotten together occasionally for dinner. We had attended the weddings of each other's children. We were both Nazarenes and had a spiritual connection. Chuck was very active in the Ontario Nazarene church.

In November of 1995 we had dinner with the class of 1951 at Point Loma University in San Diego, California. Chuck sat across from me, and we conversed all during the evening. Chuck had been an educator but is retired now. He had taught Industrial Arts for years and was very proficient in building and creating things. He now enjoys working as a handyman and is keeping extremely busy.

After the weekend at Point Loma I felt I could certainly use his talents, so I called him with a lengthy list of repair jobs in my home. He did not hesitate to come and help me.

As he worked in my home, I served him lunch, then a nice dinner, and then I even invited him to a Fourth of July barbeque at Debbie's place. He came, and later that same evening we attended the Harvest Crusade at the Angel's Stadium.

I liked Chuck and was perhaps jumping ahead of our relationship when I spotted a lovely ivory satin dress in a shop and purchased it. My thought was, "If he asks me for a date, or two or three, and eventually proposes to me, I will be ready." I never have been one to wait until the last minute for anything!

Well, we did start dating. This was August of 1996, I believe, and in November we decided, almost at the same time, that we would get married.

Chuck has two children. Rob is married to Kathy, and Christie is married to Tom. Rob and Kathy have two children, Natalie and Riley. Christie and Tom have two girls, Elizabeth and Jessica.

On February 22, 1997, we were joined as husband and wife in the Ontario Nazarene Church. There were approximately 450 people present. Our families made up the wedding party. Richard walked me down the aisle, and Debbie was my Matron of Honor. Chuck's son, Rob, was the best man, and his daughter, Christie, was the bridesmaid. My grandsons—Shad, Shane, Curtis and Brandon—were ushers, and our granddaughters— Jacquelyn, Terra, Natalie, Elizabeth and Jessica—were the flower girls. Nicole and Kim were the candle lighters. Heather attended the guest book. Pastor Larry Pitcher married us.

It was a grand day. We went to Palm Springs for our honeymoon and then on to Coronado Island for one night.

Chuck sold his home in Upland and moved in with me for a year. We then sold my home in Tustin and pooled our resources, equally coming up with a down payment for a new home, 1064 Apple Blossom Lane in Corona.

We moved to our new home on March 8, 1999. Chuck's furniture was all country, and mine was all contemporary. Needless to say, there were many discussions about what we would keep or sell or give away. We had the biggest garage sale I've ever seen.

CORONA

The new house was certainly a challenge for us. After much work, we were eventually settled.

Shane moved back with us in 1999 after many problems with jobs and cars. He eventually landed a job baking and catering at Gourmet Grubb, a small restaurant in Laguna Hills. We praise God for this. He now works for Nutri-West in Mission Viejo.

Chuck and I have been active in the Ontario Nazarene Church since our marriage and are very happy.

On August 19, 2002, my daughter, Debbie, married a wonderful Christian man named Scott Smith, who is a dentist. Scott has two children, Jeff and Keri. Debbie's business, Ambrosia Interior Design, is thriving.

Shad married darling Corinna on February 9, 2003. Corrina has a young daughter, Sarah.

How blessed I am to have these new people in my life now.

God has certainly led me through life. I cannot thank Him enough. Through it all, I praise Him who has guided, helped, strengthened, and comforted me. My earnest prayer is that all my children and grandchildren will be in heaven with me one day.

The "golden" years are now upon me. I just celebrated my 73rd birthday. Time has gone by so quickly and time has gone by so slowly, depending on the circumstances. Through the good and bad times, God has truly been with me. There has been ecstatic joy and deep sadness, but I do live the abundant life God talks about in His Word. As you probably already know, the abundant life is not the absence of pain but is the presence of God in our lives. God truly walks and talks with me. He gives me strength each day and guides my steps. I am richly blessed.

> "I will sing unto the Lord as long as I live. I will praise Him to my last breath. May He be pleased by all these thoughts about Him, for He is the source of ALL my joy" (Psalm 104:33).

The songwriter, Andrae Crouch, expresses my feelings so clearly in his songs:

> "Through it all, through it all, I've learned to trust in Jesus, I've learned to trust in God. Through it all, through it all, I've learned to depend upon His Word."

> "How can I say thanks for the things You have done for me, things so underserved You give to prove Your love for me? The voices of a million angels could not express my

gratitude. All that I am and ever hope to be, I owe it all to Thee."

TO GOD BE THE GLORY!

To be used of God
To sing, to speak, to pray
To be used of God
To show someone the way
I long so much to feel the touch
of His consuming fire
To be used of God
is my desire

About The Author

* Married 43 years to Wayne Ambrose. Raised three children and two grandsons. Presently happily married to Chuck Hart for more than six years.
* Attended five colleges: Santa Ana College, Pasadena Nazarene College, Cal State Fullerton, Long Beach State (where I received my State Teaching Credential), LaSalle University (studied interior design, and completed computer classes in 2001 in Adult Ed).
* Christian Women's Club for more than 40 years. Held several offices in the Garden Grove club, Founder and chairman of the Huntington Beach Club, Chairman of the State Conference held at the Los Angeles Marriott in 1983, Area Representative for many years, Speaker/musician from 1990 to present time.
* P.T.A. president at Clinton Elementary School, Garden Grove, 1964–1965.

* P.E.O. member and officer since 1994, helping single ladies to further their education.
* Church pianist, organist, choir director in the Bakersfield, Garden Grove and Long Beach Churches of the Nazarene since 1950; pianist at the Crystal Cathedral, 1994–1997.
* Produced a teaching video (1998) "Learn to Play the Easy Way," which sold all over the world on the Internet. Company name: Music by Hart.
* 2001—Produced a piano CD and cassette tape, "Favorite Gospel Hymns."

To order additional copies of

Grandma,
is
this
Real
Life?

Have your credit card ready and call:

1-877-421-READ (7323)

or please visit our web site at
www.pleasantword.com

Also available at: www.amazon.com

Printed in the United States
1422600002B/1-60

9 781414 100548